THE LITTLE BOOK OF
YES

By the same authors:

Yes! 60 Secrets from the Science of Persuasion

The Small Big: Small Changes that Spark Big Influence

THE LITTLE BOOK OF

YES

HOW TO WIN FRIENDS, BOOST YOUR CONFIDENCE AND PERSUADE OTHERS

NOAH GOLDSTEIN,
STEVE MARTIN AND
ROBERT CIALDINI

CURATED BY HELEN MANKIN
AND LAUREN GORDON

P

PROFILE BOOKS

First published in Great Britain in 2018 by
Profile Books Ltd
3 Holford Yard
Bevin Way
London WC1X 9HD
www.profilebooks.com

10 9 8 7 6 5 4 3 2 1

A CIP catalogue record for this book is available from the British Library.

ISBN 978 1 78816 056 8
eISBN 978 1 78283 451 9

Text design by sue@lambledesign.demon.co.uk

Printed and bound in Italy by L.E.G.O. S.p.A., Lavis (TN)

CONTENTS

PREFACE

According to John Lennon, the moment when he began to fall in love with Yoko Ono occurred at an installation of her work at the Indica Art Gallery, London, in November 1966. Among the exhibits on display, one in particular stood out. In order to view it, gallery visitors were required to climb a dimly lit, shaky ladder. Once at the top they were instructed to peer through a spyglass at a small area of the ceiling, where a single word was displayed in barely perceptible letters.

The word was small and simple yet it struck Lennon with so much force that he began to fall emotionally for the woman who arranged for him to see it. For him, the word's healing power resonated, particularly in the context of a dangerous, unstable world.

The word was not 'love,' as most people think. Instead it was a word that both leads to and flows from love, and arguably is much more obtainable within the wider array of social interactions that we all encounter.

The word was 'Yes'.

We can all recognise the enormous impact that 'Yes' can bring. 'Yes' allows relationships to blossom. It provides encouragement to learn and explore. It can mean a green light for our projects, and opportunities confirmed. 'Yes' gives us permission. And it fulfils the most basic of human motivations – our need to connect with others.

But we're all just as familiar with the frustration of hearing 'No'. Just because the word 'Yes' is a simple one, we shouldn't be fooled into believing that we can easily secure it from others. At least not without knowing about certain aspects of the persuasion process.

The Little Book of Yes contains twenty-one short chapters – each will require only five or ten minutes of your time to read – outlining a series of effective persuasion strategies. Each strategy has been proven to increase the chances that someone will agree and say 'Yes' to your request. That someone could be a colleague, a partner, a manager, a friend, even a stranger. The lessons from this book can be used to tackle a variety of everyday persuasion challenges that you might face. From repairing a soured relationship to asking for a higher fee or pay rise. From persuading someone on Twitter to see your point of view to requesting help from a neighbour or family member. From convincing a dithering friend to take action to building your social network.

Persuasion isn't magic. While some people might appear to have been born with a natural ability to influence others, that doesn't mean that the rest of us should resign ourselves to never getting our ideas or requests accepted. For decades, persuasion researchers have been studying the principles and strategies that have been shown to be universally effective at influencing others. As world-renowned persuasion scientists ourselves, we will only present ideas and principles that have been scientifically proven to increase the chances that you will be persuasive. We will talk about a variety of principles in this book, and show how to use them in effective and ethical ways. In one chapter (chapter 13, 'Complimenting') we describe the best approaches to take when dealing with a difficult colleague at work. In another (chapter 18, 'Comparing') we provide insights into the best ways to negotiate more effectively. Each of the twenty-one short and intimate chapters will show you how to apply the principles of persuasion in a variety of ways in order to win more friends, sway the undecided, boost your confidence and change the way others see you. Whether you decide to dip in and out of the book or read it cover to cover we are confident that you will learn lots of things that can result in your hearing the word 'Yes' a little more often in your personal and professional life.

One word of caution. Getting a 'Yes' once doesn't necessarily mean that you will hear it again from the same person in the future. Anyone left feeling like they have been tricked, coerced or manipulated into 'Yes' is likely to respond with its exact opposite in any subsequent interactions. So to accomplish the goal of repeated persuasive success, it is necessary to employ these insights and techniques in responsible ways. Knowing how to get to 'Yes' is a powerful tool – and this book is just the start.

We won't claim that Lennon's famous song 'All You Need Is Love' should really have been called 'All You Need Is Yes'! But we will say that if you understand and employ this book's insights in thoughtful and responsible ways, you will start to hear the word 'Yes' a lot more. In your professional life, and in your personal life too.

1

GIVING

*Giving to others is the first step to getting
what you want*

Research has long demonstrated the value of a
generous spirit. After providing gifts, favours, information and help to others, we typically become
more liked, feel more appreciated and, according to
evolutionary research, can even experience improved
physical health and feelings of well-being.

The act of giving is central to the human condition
and has a particular relevance when it comes to the
act of persuasion for a simple reason. Those who have
received help and assistance are, by and large, more
inclined to help in return if that giver ever needs assistance in the future. It is a concept that flows from the
norm of reciprocity: the social rule that demonstrates
the willingness of people to give back to others the

form of behaviour they have first received themselves.

All human societies instil this powerful social rule in their members from an early age. Your parents will almost certainly have taught you to 'treat others as you would like to be treated yourself.' Your grand-parents would undoubtedly have instructed your parents in the same way. They will have done so for a simple yet profound reason. The rule of reciprocity typically confers greater advantage to all concerned by encouraging the exchange of resources. What results is greater cooperation, increased efficiencies, and mutually beneficial and longer-lasting relationships.

Think about it. The neighbour who invites you to their party does so in the knowledge that it increases the chances that you will invite them to one of your future parties. And so the potential for a valuable and lasting relationship also increases. A colleague might feel that, by complying with a request for help on one of their co-worker's projects (by providing advice, resources or key information), their workmate will be more willing to provide help on a future project of their own. This might sound cynical – that people are really just thinking of themselves when they offer help to others. That may be true for some people, but it misses the point. Give openly and freely, and the principle of reciprocity will work by itself.

And notice that it is the act of providing help, gifts and resources to others *first* that activates the principle of reciprocity. The act of proactively giving prompts a social obligation in others to do the same. Subsequently, in the context of this social obligation, people are more inclined to say 'Yes' to a request from someone they now owe. It is the social obligations we feel towards others, rather than any conscious decision on our part, that will often result in our willingness to say yes.

Savvy marketeers recognise that even though a free sample or the trial of a new app won't persuade everyone to make a purchase, enough people will be persuaded to more than compensate them for the initial cost of their 'gift'. Charities know that including a gift in an appeal – such as a set of greeting cards – can persuade more people to make a donation. Donation rates to the American Disabled Veterans charity almost doubled when they included a sheet of personalised address labels in letters requesting financial help.

This is not to say that giving to others guarantees a return on your investment, especially if the initial offer has been so clearly contrived to be a trick. If a complete stranger approached you in the street offering money, it is unlikely that you would accept.

It's much more likely that you would recognise it for the scam it probably is.

But when giving is done with consideration and with an element of personalisation, there can be no doubting the persuasive upsides to being a willing helper and giver. In the context of an increasingly depersonalised and information-overloaded world, even relatively low levels of personalisation can be helpful. The psychologist Randy Garner found that he was able to double the number of people who would complete surveys he sent them just by accompanying his request with a short handwritten message on a Post-it note that included their name. There is a reason why you invariably open the letter from the sender who has taken the trouble to handwrite your name and address on the envelope. Unlike most communications pushed through your letterbox that compete for attention (and, in the case of bills, your cash, too), a handwritten letter stands out because someone has taken the time and trouble to personalise it. And thus it might just encourage you to take the time and trouble to respond.

When it comes to persuading others by using the rule of reciprocity, a truth emerges. Those that provide help, assistance and support first and who do so in apparently unconditional and personalised ways typically emerge as the most persuasive at work, with friends, and in their social network.

Be in no doubt, the most effective persuaders are unlikely to be people who ask themselves 'Who can help me?' They are much more likely to be those who ask themselves 'Who can I help first?'

ON GIVING

Think about someone you want to persuade, or who you want something from. What could you do or provide to help them first?

Think of ways to make your requests more personalised: could you use handwritten notes, or call someone, rather than using email?

Get into the habit of asking 'Who can I help?' rather than 'Who can help me?'

2

EXCHANGING

*Creating a culture of exchange around yourself means
everyone wins – including you!*

Have you ever noticed that if a kindly person lets you
pull out in front of them while you are queuing in
traffic there is a good chance you will extend the same
favour to another driver a short time later? Not every
time of course. And the timing is key. If more than a
few seconds elapse between being the recipient of a
traffic-related good deed and the opportunity to pass
that favour on, the odds that you will do so plummet.

Regardless of whether you do or not, it is a common
enough occurrence to be an accepted social rule. In a
way it is similar to the social rule of reciprocity. We say
similar because, strictly speaking, they're not entirely
the same thing. The work colleague who invests extra
time and resources to help you out on a project does

so in the expectation, at least to some degree, that you will return the favour and do the same for them at some point in the future. Similarly, a neighbour who takes care to watch over your flat or house while you are away on holiday can realistically expect to receive a comparable neighbourly service the next time they are away.

But when a fellow road user thoughtfully lets you pull in front of them it's hard to reciprocate given that they're now behind you. But that doesn't mean that their kind act goes unrewarded. In addition to mouthing 'thank you' as you catch their eye, or giving a thumbs up in your rear-view mirror, you are also more likely to pass the favour on to someone else. In the absence of an opportunity to give back, we *give forward* instead. It is a concept that doesn't just have upsides for the flow of traffic; it can help build relationships and more successful persuasion strategies too – with upsides for everyone concerned.

Take, by way of example, research conducted in a major telecommunications company that measured the number of favours colleagues in the office did for one another. The researchers also recorded the effect that helping others had on the helpers' social status. You won't be surprised to learn that those colleagues who were more generous with their time and assistance were viewed by their colleagues as not only more appreciated, but more likeable too. But these people were often found to be much less productive at work than their colleagues. A willingness to help others came at a cost: less time to attend to their own goals.

Fortunately, the researchers were able to identify an approach taken by a select group of employees who seemed able to provide assistance to their colleagues, boost their social status and do both these things without any detrimental effect on the achievement of their own goals. But how? Did they possess supernatural tendencies? Certainly not.

All they did was signal that the help they provided to others was part of a natural process of exchange. After being thanked for their assistance they were the kind of people who were more likely to say things like 'that's what people do for each other around here', or, 'if the situation was reversed I'm sure you'd do the same for me.' They were also much less likely to say things like 'No problem', 'Happy to help', or 'Think nothing of it'.

And they certainly, after being thanked, never, ever said 'Well, now you owe me!'

In the words of the researchers, they *arranged for*

exchange and in the process created a willing network of colleagues who became more inclined to do exactly that. Exchange means the process of giving and receiving between people in such a way that everyone benefits. Partnerships become stronger, communities are more cohesive, and cultures become more trusting and healthy.

Being a catalyst to exchange is not something that should be limited to the workplace. Sociologists have examined the most productive patterns of exchanging between families and friends. In nearly every case the happiest and healthiest environments are those where the exchange between individuals is proportionate, or equal. In circumstances where help and assistance is disproportionately provided by one or two people, levels of dissatisfaction, unhappiness and mistrust can quickly become the norm. There are several reasons why this might occur. Sometimes, helpers simply won't allow those they help to return the favour. Sometimes, even though they would welcome help, givers don't feel able to ask for it. Or perhaps receivers of help feel they will never be able to satisfy the high standards set by the giver. And at other times receivers just exploit the givers. They cease to be receivers; they are simply takers.

Of course the best way to arrange for exchange

will depend on the context. If you have a work goal that requires the assistance of others, then signalling that the previous help you provided was done in the spirit of reciprocity might be a good move. Assuming that your help was authentic and not just contrived to coerce them, then a friendly 'I really would appreciate your help' might do the trick. If your goal is a broader and less time-sensitive one, such as encouraging collaboration or information, then maybe ask the grateful recipient of your help to pay the favour forward. Ask them if you can put someone you know in touch with them, or suggest a colleague or friend who might be in need of something. Perhaps they have helpful information or an insight that would help a colleague in another department or a mutual friend.

And what of takers? Those individuals all too willing to seize the goodwill of others without a passing thought for the two-way street that defines exchange. The suggestion is that, rather than ask for help from takers, we should instead ask for their advice. When we ask takers for advice we are granting them a form of prestige. It makes them feel important and may place them in a more helpful mindset. Of course there are never guarantees when it comes to persuading others, but in the main, most people respond favourably when asked for advice.

Encouraging the paying back and forward of help and assistance could be the difference between your goals gaining momentum or being stuck in the proverbial human traffic jam.

ON EXCHANGING

If you feel that people often take advantage of you, you may be saying things like 'no problem' too often. What could you say instead?

Listen out for when people say 'thank you' to you. Keep a thank-you diary, taking care to notice whether the balance of give and take in your life is equal.

Look for ways to pay favours forward. If a colleague appreciates your help, ask if they could pass their help on to someone else in your team or network.

3

GIFTING

It really is the thought that counts – so ask people what they want, and ask for what you want

Imagine you surveyed a group of people and asked them how good they were at picking the perfect gift for, say, a friend's birthday or a colleague's retirement. What sort of responses do you think you would receive? If they are anything like the responses received by psychologists Francesca Gino and Frank Flynn when they asked this question, there's a good chance the majority of people you ask would claim to be pretty skilled gift-givers.

But if you were to follow up with another question, one that asked people how good their friends, family and work colleagues were when it came to choosing gifts, there's a good chance you would hear horror stories: from dubious hand-knitted sweaters to kitschy trinkets, to all manner of unintentionally hilarious items, including electronic singing fish. It seems that, despite claims to the contrary, if people were anywhere near as good at buying gifts as they think, then surely there would be no need for the abundance of sometimes funny, but mostly disturbing, gifts found on Pinterest and Facebook. (Search #BadGifts to be connected to thousands of examples.)

Given that the exchange of gifts is central to the rule of reciprocity, why is it that gift-givers and gift-receivers so often don't see eye to eye on the quality, usefulness and appreciation of gifts given?

In one study, researchers asked married couples to think about examples of gifts they had given as a wedding gift. Some were asked to think about gifts they had chosen from a gift registry and others were asked about gifts they had bought that were not selected from a registry. After they had given their answers the researchers turned the tables and now asked about gifts they had received on their wedding day. Similarly they were first asked about gifts they had received from their registry and then about gifts they received that were not on their registry.

The gifts that people gave were of roughly the same monetary value (they averaged about £75), and the givers assumed that the recipients appreciated them regardless of whether they were from the registry or not. However, when the couples considered the wedding gifts they themselves had received, they were far more appreciative of gifts that came from their registry list than those that did not.

In one way, this doesn't sound so surprising. Couples who are planning to get married are probably more appreciative when someone buys from a prescribed list that contains items they need for a new home – items that they wouldn't wish to miss out on or duplicate. After all, who needs three cheese boards? Or two singing fish?

But what happens when the gift-giving context is different? What if the gift is for a birthday rather than a wedding? When the researchers tested this in some additional studies they found the exact same pattern. Gift-givers didn't think that their recipients' level of happiness and appreciation for a gift would matter much as a function of whether the recipient asked for the gift or not. But in reality people were much happier and much more appreciative when they received something that they had previously said they would like.

So, is a simple solution when it comes to choosing the perfect gift to just ask friends and family to write down what they might like and then buy something for them from the list?

Actually, yes!

But this approach also raises a concern. Does having to ask a friend what they want signal that, as the giver, you don't know them well enough to buy a personalised gift? Or, worse still, will they think that you can't be bothered spending the time, effort or energy necessary to choose a suitable gift?

It turns out these concerns are unfounded. Those who receive gifts they asked for are actually far more appreciative because they were given something they really wanted. And the level of appreciation that people feel for the gifts we give them is important. Not only is it one of the main determinants of how much people might be motivated to reciprocate in the future, it also effects their happiness too. So, when choosing gifts for others, finding ways of identifying what someone truly wants and then buying it is a win-win for everyone involved. An appreciative and happy recipient. A relieved and happy giver.

So how much should you spend on a gift? We have come to learn that, typically in life, you get what you pay for. As a result, does the amount you spend on a gift matter? The answer is yes, but perhaps not in the way that you think. High gift prices are not always a sign of appreciated gifts. In certain circumstances, less can seem like a lot more.

In one study, when researchers presented people with two gifts – a relatively cheap wool coat (it cost £55) and a relatively expensive scarf (it cost £45) – receivers rated the generosity of the scarf-giver much, much higher despite the fact that their gift cost less, providing a helpful tip for any gift-giver. If you want to be known among your friends and family as a thoughtful and generous gift-giver (while secretly remaining a thrifty one too) the advice is to purchase high-value gifts from low-value product categories (like the £45 scarf) rather than low-value gifts from high-value categories. Doing so provides several advantages. Recipients of your gifts will feel more appreciated. Your perceived generosity rises. And, perhaps most important of all, you avoid the risk of being labelled 'cheap'!

ON GIFTING

Remember, it's OK to ask people what they want.
They will end up happier and so will you.

Which means that it is perfectly OK to tell people what you want, too.

Next time you buy something for anyone – whether it's a bottle of wine or a birthday gift – remember that price is relative – it's better to buy something of high quality than high price.

4

COOPERATING

Thinking 'we' rather than 'you vs me' will bring people to your side in more ways than one

In December 1914, Europe remained locked in the bloodiest struggle it had ever known. The opposing armies along the Western Front were in close proximity; in many places they were within shouting distance. And as weeks stretched into months, the soldiers became increasingly familiar with their equivalents in the opposite trenches.

Gradually, cooperation between the two sides became more prevalent. This began with enemy troops deliberately holding their fire so that comrades could retrieve the bodies of their fallen soldiers during the night.

These ceasefires laid the foundations for the legendary Christmas Truce of World War I. The story goes, for a few hours on Christmas Day, 1914, the troops on either side of the enemy lines declared a spontaneous ceasefire. Soldiers came out of their trenches and would-be adversaries came together to play a game of football.

When individuals, or even enemies, come together in order to reach common goals it can seem at odds with what many people assume is a dog-eat-dog evolutionary mentality. It's no wonder that the Christmas Truce has become one of the most famous stories of war. In a world where conflict and collaboration seem diametrically opposed, it's an inspiring story of an interlude among troops showing how even bitter foes can work out rituals of cooperation.

It might seem hard: we tend to think of ourselves as separate from others. We often think in terms of 'You' and 'Me' or 'Them' and 'Us', caught in tribe mentalities where it's everyone for themselves. But cooperation is crucial to persuasion. And if we focus on what binds rather than divides us then it becomes much easier to cooperate, and eventually to persuade. Think 'We' rather than 'You' vs 'Me'.

This was the case with the Christmas Truce. It was the common identity of being soldiers and a common love of football that led, at least for a while, to cooperation between enemies. And finding areas in which to cooperate and highlighting shared interest is still just as powerful today.

In a wonderful series of studies, British psychologist Mark Levine asked groups of staunch Manchester United supporters to complete a questionnaire asking what they liked about their team, before asking them to walk to a second building in order to complete the next stage of the study. En route they witnessed someone (who was part of the study) tripping over and supposedly injuring themselves. Sometimes the injured party would be wearing a plain white shirt, sometimes a Manchester United shirt and, at others times, the shirt of a rival club.

Strategically placed observers, clipboards at the ready, stood by to count how many supporters stopped to help. Just over a third helped when the injured person wore a plain white T-shirt, but wearing a Manchester United shirt persuaded the overwhelming majority to help. Perhaps unsurprisingly, the injured party fared worst when wearing the shirt of a rival: clear evidence of people's tendency to mostly help those whom they see as belonging to their in-group.

Fortunately, the studies also demonstrate that people aren't typically so narrow-minded that they can't be persuaded to cooperate more with those they initially see as outsiders: when the study was repeated and Manchester United supporters were first asked what they liked about being football supporters, rather than just what they liked about their team, they became twice as likely to help someone wearing a rival shirt.

In the Christmas Truce of World War I, it is probable that after months of futile fighting, many of the troops had come to see the men behind the enemy lines as similar to themselves, part of a wider identity of 'wearied troops' rather than British vs German soldiers. And, while the sorts of challenges that *you* might face in persuading people to cooperate with each other pale in comparison, the basic rules of engagement remain the same. Focus on the common goals that bind rather than divide you, the larger identity that you share. Look for a point that both parties can agree upon first, and make that central to your discussion. It is an approach that seems obvious, yet it's one that can frequently be missed in the heat of the moment.

Another effective way to build cooperative connections between yourself and others is to actively invite them to collaborate with you. Suppose you've come up with a good idea at work. Rather than go it alone in an attempt to win all the acclaim, the advice is instead to develop a draft of your plan and then give it to a colleague or even your boss and ask for their input. By arranging that buy-in you have also arranged for their cooperation and, importantly, their ownership. It is a strategy often dubbed the IKEA effect, so named because people place a much higher value on things they have partially created – rather like that wonky cabinet you or your partner constructed from a flat-pack kit.

ON COOPERATING

Next time you have a project or proposal you want to pitch, say to your boss, 'I'd really love to get your input on this.' Gaining their input creates a convergence of ideas and is a key step in successful persuasion.

When dealing with stand-offish colleagues or neighbours try to find out what you have in common and highlight that before trying to persuade them.

Do a quick search on LinkedIn or Facebook before meeting someone for the first time and look for shared interests and common experiences.

Look at chapter 2, 'Exchanging', to see the usefulness of asking for advice: advice leads to a perception of partnership, teamwork and, ultimately, cooperation.

5

PAUSING

Emotion affects all our interactions so take a moment to check in with yourself before attempting to influence others

If you are a fan of the TV series *Sex and the City* you may remember an episode in which Carrie Bradshaw is walking down a New York City street with her close friend Samantha who is nursing an injured foot, causing her to limp along. 'Ow!' Samantha cries out at one point, causing her sympathetic friend to reply, 'Honey, if it hurts so much, why are we going shopping?'

'I have a broken toe, not a broken spirit,' comes the retort.

Many will sympathise. Lots of people use shopping as a way to seek solace and alleviate sorrow. But this isn't necessarily wise. We will all recognise times when our emotional state has influenced our behaviour and choices detrimentally, perhaps even to the extent that we have ended up making decisions that at the time seemed right, but have ended up costing much more in the long run.

When it comes to persuasion, it is important to recognise the important role that emotions play. There is a lot of research that looks at the role of emotions in decision making, particularly when it comes to purchasing and negotiating. For example, the experience of sadness can have a major impact on how much people are prepared to pay for things: sad buyers are often willing to pay a higher price for items than neutral buyers, and sad sellers are often willing to part with items for a lower price than neutral sellers. In one study, people were asked to watch one of two films: one an emotionally charged movie that induced a feeling of sadness in viewers and the other a neutrally emotive film about … fish.

Afterwards, they were divided into two groups. One group was asked to give a price at which they would be willing to buy a range of different products. The other group was asked to set a price at which they would sell them. Sad buyers were willing to spend around 30 per cent *more* than emotionally neutral buyers. And sad sellers were willing to part with about a third *less* than were their emotionally neutral partners. It would seem that these decisions were occurring completely outside anyone's awareness. No one had any idea they had been so deeply affected by these residual feelings of sadness.

Of course, sadness isn't the only emotion that can affect your ability to make your case, or persuade others. All emotions can. Think about a time when you have been excited about an opportunity. Under such circumstances there is a tendency to focus too much on the upsides and fail to spot the risks that could be faced. On the other hand, if you're feeling anxious you might focus too much on what could go wrong and end up passing up a really good offer. Where all other things are equal, it is the emotionally neutral decision makers who tend to make the better decisions.

So it is really important to identify the emotional state you are in before making important decisions, starting a crucial negotiation or even responding to an unfriendly email. From negotiating the terms of your contract with the phone company, to buying a new home or having a job interview, your emotions will be involved. If you are experiencing heightened emotions, and even though you might believe that your decision-making ability will be unaffected, you should consider holding off interacting with others.

It can be hard to do, but a short pause to compose yourself can help. As emotions subside, your ability to think clearly, and make your points persuasively, will increase.

At work, if you are the sort of person who schedules meetings back to back, without giving yourself time in between them, then you may be doing yourself a disservice. The advice is to schedule a short break in between. That way you'll reduce the likelihood that any feelings generated by one meeting will spill over into the next. This could be especially important if the next meeting involves making significant decisions or a crucial negotiation.

The same is true with friends and family. Entering into a discussion in a frustrated, anxious, angry or otherwise unhelpful emotional state can quickly turn a seemingly simple exchange of opinions into an argument where persuasion and influence becomes impossible.

Be aware too, when seeking to influence others' decisions, of the role that their mood plays. Attempting to persuade someone who has just received unsettling news, or, worse still, reminding someone of a topic that you know will put them in a gloomy mood, is both unwise and at times even morally wrong. If you use their negative emotions to prompt people into making decisions, it will often lead to regret and resentment, and do little to build long-term relationships. In fact, by offering to postpone negotiating with someone who has just had a negative experience, you'll actually strengthen your relationship. You'll seem nobler, more caring and wise.

All priceless characteristics of anyone who wishes to hear the word 'Yes' a little more.

ON PAUSING

Before important meetings and interactions, ask yourself: 'What state of mind am I in right now?' If it is an unhelpful one, then pause to let those feelings subside.

Find ways to guard against strong emotions interrupting your meetings. Get some fresh air beforehand. Talk a short walk. Be still for a moment. Try to create separation from an unhelpful emotional state.

When asking someone for something, make sure that it's a good time – if they seem upset, angry or troubled, come back later.

6

COMPROMISING

First requests can significantly influence the success of later ones – so start with a high demand and then compromise

Imagine, one day, as you are walking along the street, you are approached by someone who, except for greeting you with a friendly smile, appears otherwise entirely unremarkable. They introduce themselves as a member of a local youth worker institute, and enquire whether you would be willing to help the centre by volunteering to escort a group of children on a trip to the zoo this weekend. Thinking of your planned weekend activities and, doing your best to avoid eye contact, you politely decline. You might think that the youth centre workers have got their work cut out persuading people to sign up to such a scheme. And you would be right. The scenario painted here was in fact a study. Results showed that only a small minority of people approached for help were willing to say 'Yes' to the request.

But on the other side of the road a different group of youth workers are also approaching passers-by. This group has discovered a way to triple the number of people who are willing to chaperone a group of children to the zoo that weekend. Their strategy doesn't require any costly incentives, or targeting a particular type of person. Instead, all their strategy requires of them is a basic understanding of the psychology of human compromise.

'Would you be willing to become a counsellor at the centre?' they would ask people, before going on to explain that this would involve an investment of two hours of their time, each weekend, on a programme that lasted for the next three years. Imagine people's reactions when presented with such a request. Lots of firm and sometimes even very blunt refusals.

No one was willing to sign up. But then something surprising happened.

Undeterred by the initial rejection, the youth workers then instantly offered a compromise. 'I understand how big a commitment volunteering for a three-year programme is. So how about you take a few kids to the zoo this weekend instead?'

The result? A three-fold increase in the number of people who said 'Yes'.

What this study and others like it have found is that, when it comes to agreeing to requests, people are often much more likely to say 'Yes' to a smaller request immediately after they have said 'No' to a larger one. One reason for this common phenomenon is that people typically view concessions and compromises as a gift of sorts. In chapter 1, 'Giving', we explored the idea that people – in line with the rule for reciprocity – feel a social obligation to give back to others what they have been provided with first. It seems that the human response to social obligation doesn't just apply to gifts, favours and free samples. It applies to concessions and compromises too.

This strategy (referred to by social psychologists as the *rejection then retreat* approach) is most effective when the first request made is not so extreme as to appear implausible. Initial requests that are deliberately inflated so that a lesser request 'appears' more acceptable are likely to be seen for the obvious trick they are and then rejected. That is not to say, however, that you shouldn't make bold initial requests. In fact a common mistake that people make when attempting to persuade others is to fail to ask for their ideal scenario. All too often, probably in an attempt to avoid an outright refusal, people will reduce what they would ideally wish for and, in doing so, reduce their overall persuasiveness in two ways.

First, people might actually say 'Yes' to your opening request. Not always, but certainly sometimes. And certainly always more than to a request they have never been presented with. Second, and in line with the *rejection then retreat* effect, a subsequent compromise request immediately becomes more likely to be acquiesced to. So if you start small, you might end up small. Or even smaller.

Note the word *immediately*. It may sound obvious but it is something that is regularly forgotten. After an initial request or proposal is rejected we often retreat to lick our wounds prior to working out an alternative to return with on another day. In doing so, we miss our moment of persuasive power. Those requests, that we see as subsequent, are more likely to be seen as separate by those to whom we are making them. It's unlikely that asking people to take a group of kids to the zoo will succeed a couple of days after those same people have rejected the bigger commitment of becoming long-term counsellors. Those being approached are more likely to see the requester as an annoyance.

ON COMPROMISING

Ask yourself: 'What is my ideal goal and what would I be prepared to accept as a compromise?' Be prepared and know in advance what you want, and what you'd settle with.

Your ideal goal should always be your opening proposal.

Avoid the temptation to reduce your opening request in the belief that it will be rejected. The word 'No' is your friend in situations like these. Be bold and make a second request.

7

KNOWING

Demonstrating your expertise and knowledge before you start speaking will make sure that people listen

A critical tool to being persuasive is having knowledge or expertise. Even if you aren't the most senior person in the room, you can still sway the debate by demonstrating that you have certain expertise, the right facts, and that you have done your research. But maybe you have found yourself in a position where you are clearly the most qualified or knowledgeable person but don't speak for fear of being branded a know-it-all. Maybe your good ideas and insights go under-recognised by colleagues in meetings, leading to someone else's lesser idea winning the day.

Hermione Granger was no stranger to this situation during her time at Hogwarts. She was often heckled by her fellow classmates for having the right answer, and in one particular Defence against the Dark Arts class, she was left embarrassed and upset by the professor's nasty remark: 'Miss Granger, do you take pride in being an insufferable know-it-all?'

When you find yourself in a position like Hermione, where you *do* know best and want to share your knowledge for the benefit of everyone but at the same time don't want people to stop listening or dismiss you as a show-off, what should you do? It turns out that there is an answer.

No matter how hard they tried to persuade their patients to accept that to be healthier they needed to exercise more, most nurses in one particular hospital found that few of their patients would comply. This didn't seem to be case with their colleagues, the doctors. Why were the doctors able to get patients to listen? Maybe the title of 'Doctor' makes a difference? To find out, they did something ingenious. They decided to pin their diplomas, certifications and awards on the walls of their consulting rooms. Did their patients react by thinking that this group of nurses was a bunch of show-offs? Absolutely not. They reacted by exercising more. About 30 per cent more, in fact.

By displaying their qualifications on the wall the nurses could be seen by their patients for what they really were: genuinely credible, knowledgeable experts. The result? A huge improvement in patient compliance. Why? Because people look to experts to show them the way, and subtle cues in the environment, like diplomas on walls, can help identify those experts.

The answer, then, is to be *subtle*. Had the nurses flaunted their certificates to their patients in order to show what they knew, they could have been seen as ego-driven rather than expertise-driven. Having the evidence of their qualifications visible was all that was needed in order to communicate the worth of their advice. The same will be true for you. Finding ways to introduce your expertise before you speak can change an audiences' reaction to what you say. So make sure that qualifications and your job title appear in the signature of your email. Include your degree on business cards together with membership of any trade or professional bodies. Update your LinkedIn profile and include case studies and examples of the latest projects you are involved in. Make sure that your personal website has a link to your CV. Perhaps even consider submitting an article to a trade magazine or a blog on a website that's followed by your industry colleagues.

There are times, of course, when it might be tricky to show what you know: when presenting in front of an audience, for example, or pitching an idea to a roomful of colleagues. Asking your audience to review your impressive yet self-promoting brag file before listening to what you have to say seems unlikely to work. It may convey your expertise, but might also be perceived as boastful. With forthright self-promotion out of the question, what can you do to demonstrate your credibility and expertise?

One option is to get someone to introduce you. This approach has been widely practised for many years by speakers and performers, where it is customary for a communicator to be introduced prior to their presentation. It might only be a few lines (you can easily write them yourself) but it can work wonders in setting the scene and getting your audience receptive to the important messages about to come. You also avoid the damage that blatant self-flattery can result in. If pitching with a business partner for a tender or for a client's project, ask your partner to introduce you first – and then return the favour. When sending a pitching email include written endorsements from previous clients.

A group of estate agents arranged for receptionists who answered customer enquiries to inform them of their colleagues' expertise. 'Let me put you through to Sandra in sales' became 'I'm going to put you through to Sandra, our head of sales, who has over fifteen years' experience selling properties.' The number of appointments and the number of signed contracts rose dramatically.

The point is that it isn't always necessary to be in the driving seat to direct the car. Presenting yourself as *knowledgeable* by arranging for your expertise on the subject at hand to be known before you speak can persuade others to turn in your direction.

ON KNOWING

Wherever possible, arrange for someone else to introduce you.

If that isn't possible, send your biography or profile in advance of any meeting.

Include qualifications and experience at the very top of your CV. Never hide them away at the end.

8

ADMITTING

By being upfront about the downsides in your ideas you can increase your authenticity and your persuasiveness

According to the ancient Japanese philosophy wabi-sabi, to have weaknesses is to be beautiful. Wabi-sabi is the aesthetic world view of finding and appreciating the beauty in imperfection, impermanence and incompletion.

Anyone who has ever grown their own vegetables, built furniture from scratch or simply baked cookies will recognise that there is beauty in imperfection. The crooked but home-grown carrot. The chair that leans slightly to one side. The oddly shaped chocolate chip cookies with their uneven, textured edges. Given that we often assign a disproportionately high value to things we have created ourselves, we are more likely to accept such things as they are – flaws and all.

Rarely, however, does a willingness to accept and even find beauty in the weaknesses of an object extend to our own imperfections and weaknesses. A case in point is the job interview. Most candidates, perhaps understandably, approach these nerve-jangling moments hoping to impress would-be employers with as close to a perfect account of their skills and expertise as possible. The task at hand is to come out on top by appearing a perfect fit for the role. No place for rough edges here.

But savvy employers know this – which is why they will often ask candidates about their weaknesses. Keen to avoid disclosing their greatest flaws, candidate responses to this question, such as an admittance to being 'a perfectionist' or 'a workaholic' are common-place. This is not the time, the thinking goes, to candidly reveal yourself, warts and all.

Or is it?

Psychological research suggests that, rather than undermine our position, under certain circumstances a willingness to be upfront about our weaknesses can serve to place us in a position of power.

A classic experiment conducted some fifty years ago demonstrates not only the counter-intuitiveness of this idea, but also its continued relevance in today's arguably more complex and uncertain world. In the experiment, people were asked to listen to recordings of two people who were answering questions in a quiz. One person would routinely answer around nine out of the ten questions correctly. The other would get about half right. After hearing the recording, listeners were asked to rate the quiz-takers' competence and likeability. No surprise that the person who aced the quiz was rated as more competent and likeable than the person who was wrong half the time.

But here's where the study gets interesting. Some participants were told that, while answering questions, the quiz ace had, rather embarrassingly, managed to spill coffee over themselves. Upon hearing of this blunder, the rating of competence and likeability awarded by listeners to the strong quiz performer increased even further. But when informed that it was the poorer performer who had spilt coffee, the likeability and competence rating for that person fell through the floor.

It seems that admitting a mistake can provide superior performers with an additional boost to their likeability (we will have more to say about being likeable in chapter 12). But that same action negatively impacts lesser performers. Psychologists call this the pratfall effect. It describes how the attractiveness of a person increases after they admit a mistake, but only if they are relatively competent in the first place.

So it would appear that there are strengths to be gained through weaknesses. No one is perfect. Everyone knows this. So embracing your smaller weaknesses can lead to big boosts in your impact and influence. Depending, of course, on the type of weakness that is disclosed. Spilling coffee over yourself is a common and relatively minor flaw that will mark you down as someone who is human. But admitting during a job interview that you spilt coffee over a former boss or, worse still, over the company server, leading to an IT outage, is likely to be considered a much bigger error and detrimental to your case.

So the advice when seeking to have an impact on others is to be a willing confessor of little faults. Doing so can help demonstrate that you make mistakes just like everyone else. By declaring a small weakness openly at the beginning of an interaction, we increase an audience's perception of our authenticity, honesty, trustworthiness and reliability. It also means that the other person relaxes, and is more likely to listen to us. So in job interviews a good approach is to admit a genuine but minor weakness that won't necessarily be detrimental and can be improved by taking action. It can also be a good idea to proactively mention an area of your personal development that you are motivated to work on rather than wait for the interviewer to ask that dreaded question … 'Tell me about your weaknesses.'

As the wabi-sabi philosophy suggests, weaknesses are not blemishes that need to be masked but are, rather, an aspect of ourselves that can be character-building or may serve to humanise us in the eyes of others. They can be as appealing as the pages of a well-thumbed book, a chipped teacup or a patch on your jumper.

ON ADMITTING

In order to embrace your small flaws you need to be aware of them. Make a (short) list of yours.

If you find that hard, or don't think you possess any flaws, ask a friend or partner who may see something that is invisible to you.

Don't be afraid to admit to mistakes or small bad habits – but don't begin confessing all your guilty secrets!

9

ASKING

Sometimes getting what we want is less about persuading, and more a matter of just asking

Benjamin Franklin, one of the Founding Fathers of the United States of America, was a man of many talents. During his life he turned his considerable skills to a variety of endeavours: he was an author, printer, postmaster, inventor and humorist. These in addition to being a civic activist, politician, statesman and diplomat.

He was a pretty good persuader too – something he would often attribute to his willingness to ask for help.

A story that he was fond of telling was how he once won favour with a political adversary by writing to him asking to borrow a rare and valuable book. A short time afterwards Franklin reported that this usually stubborn, often hostile gentleman sought him out in the House and spoke graciously and respectfully to him for the first time.

Franklin's wisdom was to recognise that, in certain circumstances, asking for help can be an effective way of building bridges with people. And, ultimately, persuading them to your side.

But what if you're not Benjamin Franklin? What if you are a normal person who worries about soliciting assistance from an icy-faced work colleague? Or someone who struggles doggedly in pursuit of a task sooner than ask for help from a grumpy next-door neighbour or family member? And what of other kinds of 'ask-related' situations, like plucking up the courage to ask that cute guy or girl on the bus, who you've admired from a distance, out for coffee?

For many, asking is a daunting prospect. So here is some good news; if you are the kind of person who considers asking to be a risky business – one laced with the fear of rejection and a potential for embarrassment – then reassurance is at hand. Countless scientific studies have demonstrated the empowering, often liberating, qualities of asking.

The respected psychologists Frank Flynn and Vanessa Bohns have conducted numerous studies looking at many different types of request: soliciting charitable donations, asking to borrow a stranger's phone, even asking people to fill out lengthy questionnaires. In each case they first ask people to predict the likelihood that those they ask will agree to their request.

In most cases people underestimate their success rate – by around half.

One of the reasons why we typically underestimate the chances that someone will say 'Yes' to our requests concerns what we focus on. Requesters tend to think about the economic costs that people will incur if they do say 'Yes' to us, like their time. In contrast, potential helpers are much more likely to think about the social costs of saying 'No'. A simple truth emerges. People are far more likely to say 'Yes' than we expect. The result of not asking? Business opportunities lost. Potential clients un-contacted. Networking opportunities wasted.

In addition to underestimating the odds that people will say 'Yes' to our requests, many people believe that asking for help weakens your position. But again, this is often a misperception.

We've all been a passenger in a car driven by someone (probably a guy) who'll travel miles in the wrong direction rather than stop and ask for directions. Perhaps they believe that asking for help is a sign of weakness. But that momentary feeling of weakness (admitting you're lost) is actually the route to a far more powerful position. In the case of the lost driver, that's access to crucial help and assistance that gets them back on track to their destination.

So rather than seeing it as limiting, it's actually far more productive to view asking for help as empowering. This should serve as comforting, especially to those in difficult situations – folks in financial difficulties, the victims of bullying or harassment – who may feel that they will be stigmatised for seeking assistance.

Even the student who raises a hand and asks what they believe might be a silly question increases their power in two ways. First, they will probably gain the extra information needed to allow for an important learning. Second, they'll also gain the thanks of their classmates, many of whom are also stuck, but who failed to ask. Those classmates are subsequently more likely to feel some sense of obligation and reciprocity towards their fellow student.

If you still aren't convinced of the tremendous power of asking for help, then perhaps the studies conducted by Thomas Gilovich and Victoria Husted Medvec, and published in the *Journal of Personality and Social Psychology*, might change your mind. Gilovich and Medvec find that for most people there is a temporal pattern to the regret of not taking action. Put more simply, any awkwardness, embarrassment or pain that might be felt as a result of asking for help or having a request refused tends to be acute and temporary. Rather like a bee sting, it smarts for a few minutes, but rapidly subsides.

In contrast, the regret that one feels for not asking is entirely different. Unlike a momentary pinprick it tends to be more of a dull ache that hangs around much longer. Like a broken record repeatedly playing 'if only ...' in your head.

With so many reassuring pluses on the side of asking, maybe the time has come to reach out to that icy-faced work colleague or grumpy neighbour. Sure, it will require a little bravery. A little courage. Maybe even the welcome support of a stiff G&T. But surely it's worth a try.

ON ASKING

Over a week, keep a record of the numbers of 'Yeses' and 'Nos' your direct requests receive – you'll soon notice the impact of asking.

Remember that a short sting of possible embarrassment is a small price to pay compared to the lingering ache of 'if only'.

Next time you want something – ask for it.

10

CONVERSING

When it comes to successful influence, it's good to talk

Humans are the most social of all creatures. When we feel involved and connected to others our feelings of well-being soar. In contrast, when we are isolated or marginalised we feel unhappy. So it's perhaps puzzling that, in environments where lots of people are present, and given the benefits of connecting with others, we often value isolation more highly.

Take conferences, networking events or even drink receptions in a bar or hotel lobby. Are you the sort who prefers to keep yourself to yourself? Or are you a more 'out there' kind of person? Someone who seeks out connections with others. Always alert to the possibility of meeting interesting new people. People who, if you're lucky, might turn into useful contacts, even future friends.

If you have more in common with the latter, then congratulations. The chances are that your conversational skills are serving to increase your ability to build relationships, networks and, by association, your influence too. You are also probably in a minority.

The fact is that most people are minded to keep themselves to themselves. If this describes you, then you might be interested to learn about research that clearly demonstrates the considerable upsides of reaching out to others. In short, if you want to increase your network and potential future opportunities the advice is clear – get chatting.

But starting a conversation with a complete stranger is hard, right? It might even be risky. And doing so certainly goes against the grain of a lot of social norms. There are a couple of reasons for this.

The psychological concept known as *infrahumanisation* is a long name for a simple idea, which states that people often carry the belief that others are somehow slightly less human than they are. This may sound both alarming and self-regarding, yet, from a certain perspective, it also makes sense. We clearly have better access to our own thoughts, desires, intentions and behaviours than we do those of others. So when we face an opportunity to initiate a conversation with a potentially impolite and unpredictable stranger, we'll usually choose isolation over inclusion. And we'll be largely unaware of the fact that they're probably thinking the exact same thing.

Of course another possibility is that if we do bite the bullet and start talking to a stranger we might quickly find out that they are, in fact, quite unpleasant. Or, worse still, they might think that we are!

Technology has a role to play too. Today, with so many technology-based opportunities to connect with others, it is easy to overlook the value of the real-life, personal connection, the most basic of all.

Regardless of the reasons for our reluctance to engage with unknown others face-to-face, studies by behavioural scientists offer compelling evidence of the considerable upsides available to those that do.

In one experiment, commuters were approached at a train station on their way to work. Importantly, the stations selected were at the start of the rail line, meaning that the passengers would be boarding a relatively empty train and would therefore be more likely to choose a seat away from other commuters (the norm) rather than choosing one next to a stranger. After agreeing to take part in the study, some travellers were asked to strike up a conversation with a stranger on their journey to work during which they should attempt to find out something interesting about them and to tell them something about themselves. Another group of commuters were explicitly asked to keep to themselves during their journey and to enjoy the solitude. Everyone in the study was given a survey to complete and send back at the end of their journey.

From trains to buses, waiting rooms to airport lounges, a common pattern emerged. The people asked to make a connection with a stranger reported that they had had a significantly more positive journey experience compared to those who were asked to seek solitude. Conversations lasted, on average, around fourteen minutes and were rated as pleasant, which was in direct contrast to how commuters predicted they would feel if they did connect with a stranger. Many also thought that attempting to start a conversation with a fellow commuter posed a high risk of social rejection. But, and in keeping with what we discovered in chapter 9, 'Asking', none of the 118 commuters in the study who made conversation with a stranger were ever rebuffed.

You may be thinking that, rather than an opportunity for chatting, travel is a chance to catch up with emails, read a report or carry out other work-related activities. But the researchers found that initiating a conversation with a fellow commuter didn't come at any significant cost to productivity.

It's a lesson that applies well beyond a travel context. The same strategy can equally be used in more traditional networking environments such as conferences, meetings, events and bars. We're often tempted to fill those empty moments before a talk begins, or an event starts. But next time you have the opportunity, put down your iPhone, report, Kindle or computer and start a conversation with the person next to you. It is one immediate way to increase the number of people in your network, establish greater connections and, in turn, broaden your persuasiveness. Be comforted that rejections are actually quite rare provided that the first few moments of an exchange are focused on getting to know the person and seeking interesting facts about them.

ON CONVERSING

Next time you are on a plane, a bus or at conference and the person next to you isn't looking down at their phone or otherwise occupied, try saying 'hello'.

Practise 'introducing yourself' in front of a mirror – remember eye contact and a genuine smile.

When dining with friends, encourage more conversation by agreeing to place mobile phones in the centre of the table. Whoever looks at their phone first (a sign that a Facebook update or tweet is more important than the people at the table) pays for dinner!

11

HUMANISING

When it comes to persuading audiences, stories trump facts and humanity beats statistics

The India–Pakistan partition in the summer of 1947 tore friends, families and communities apart overnight. For a young boy named Baldev, this signalled no more flying kites with his friend Yusuf. Baldev would be moving far away from Lahore with little hope of ever seeing his friend again.

Sixty-six years later, Baldev sits with his grand-daughter in one of India's cafés, looking through an old scrapbook crammed full of faded photographs of his childhood and his long-lost friend.

Looking at the old man, his granddaughter decides that she is going to find Yusuf. Her tenacity and persistence, coupled with some ingenious online investigation, leads her to discover that Yusuf has a grandson.

She makes contact and, together, they hatch their plan.

Hearing a knock at the door, Baldev answers. He does not immediately recognise his friend. 'Happy birthday, my old friend,' answers a familiar voice, triggering a powerful embrace fuelled by six decades of separation. The resourceful grandchildren look on, tears in eyes, as they witness the emotional reunion of old friends divided by borders but united by humanity.

This is a heart-warming anecdote about an otherwise tragic period of Indian–Pakistani history. But it is also something else. It is a scene-by-scene description of a Google ad that positions its search engine as the channel for discovery and connection. Rather than use facts and statistics to get across their message, Google exploited a fundamental truth that persuasion scientists and ad-men have known for decades. When it comes to persuading audiences, stories trump facts and humanity beats statistics.

The persuasive impact of humanising is evident in domains far beyond advertising. Smart politicians craft 'stories' for their campaigns. They recognise that it's far easier to connect voters to their policy ideas through the story of, say, a single mother pushed into poverty, than communicate their detailed plans to tackle benefit reform. The very best teachers are recognised as storytellers first, educators second. From political speeches to TED talks, successful persuaders understand that the provision of information and facts rarely moves an audience. But stories about people do. The humanising of a message or proposal can frequently crowd out any amount of objective information and data. This is the case even when you would expect an audience to be especially receptive to information and data.

Take medicine, for example, a career in which practitioners pride themselves on being well-informed and objective, with the noble goal of providing their patients with access to the same medical treatments and levels of care regardless of condition, status or social class. But people can become dulled by their jobs – even doctors or consultants. What if doctors were reminded that the data they study relates to real people?

A rather unusual medical study investigated this very question. Would doctors become more 'caring', that is, would they conduct a more thorough analysis of a patient's condition, order more tests and detect more abnormalities, if a patient's photograph was simply attached to an X-ray or CT scan compared to when it wasn't? By all accounts the answer is yes. And by a significant amount. Another demonstration of the persuasive power that comes from humanising information.

So why does the humanisation of a message change our attitudes, beliefs and reaction to it? Why do we so often become putty in the hands of an accomplished storyteller? Psychologists argue that when we are exposed to arguments based on logic and fact it is easier to be naturally dubious and critical about what is being said. But humanising messages radically alters the way information is processed. Stories transport audiences, allowing them to form connections with the people in the narrative and, subsequently, to become more receptive to the claims of the underlying message. In fact, humanising messages and appeals can overwhelm audiences to the extent that their ability to detect inaccuracies and missteps in what is presented is often reduced. It seems that in addition to becoming emotionally moved we can also become intellectually defenceless.

When persuading others, the lesson is clear. Attempting to influence and persuade through the use of a dispassionate presentation of data, costs and benefits goes against the grain of our emotional state. So when making a case, don't just talk in terms of cold hard facts. Talk in terms of warmer, softer human stories too. Why should your boss care about that new initiative you are proposing? How will it change the world or affect lives? How will people feel when it is completed?

The route to persuading one mind, your entire office, your family or the whole world, invariably, it would seem, is a human one.

ON HUMANISING

When you are clear about your goal, find a story that will bring it to life and make it desirable to others.

Think about what makes a good story – find characters your audience can identify with, and show their motivation and desires.

Wherever possible, use pictures of people as well as, or instead of, charts and spreadsheets in order to convey your message.

12

LIKING

To get someone to agree with you, get them to like you first

'Opposites attract', 'Birds of a feather flock together': doubtless both of these sayings will be familiar to you. You probably have an example, perhaps several examples, that readily come to mind where each has been true. You might recall a couple you met at a party who stand out in your memory because of how different they were to each other. Nonetheless, you easily explain their relationship by telling yourself (and others) that opposites attract. Maybe at the same party you meet another couple. They finish each other's sentences, and mirror each other's mannerisms. When you see them you immediately decide that not only *are* they together, they are *meant* to be together. They are the birds of a feather, who flocked together.

Neither of these situations is surprising. We can think of examples of where opposites attract as easily as we can think about examples of 'flocking, similar' others. But these things are very different. One suggests that people feel more positively towards others to the extent that they are similar. The other argues that people will like each other to the extent that they are different. So which is it? Birds of a feather? Or opposites?

To answer this question we need to go back to the summer of 1993 and to the town of Quincy, Illinois, situated on the banks of the Mississippi River. It is a small town. Only around forty thousand people live there. It is affectionately known as Gem City. Not because of its hidden diamond and ruby mines. There are none. But because of the fertile lands that brought prosperity to its early dwellers.

In the summer of 1993 the Mississippi flooded to devastating effect. Several towns and cities were ruinously impacted. Quincy was one of them. In response, hundreds of residents worked night and day shifting thousands of sandbags in order to build barriers against rising tides. Things looked bleak. Power supplies and sources of food were steadily declining. Fatigue and pessimism were rising as fast as, maybe faster than the water levels themselves. In those dark moments any shred of good news made the appalling situation, if only for a few moments, a little brighter. One of those brighter moments came in the form of a large donation from the residents' association of another city, located over a thousand miles away in Massachusetts.

Why would a random city located 1,000 miles away act so generously towards a town few, if any, of its residents would have known or heard of? And why only help Quincy? Many other cities and towns were impacted by the floods. Why didn't they benefit from this New England generosity? There is an intriguing answer. It concerns a shared name. The city in Massachusetts was also called Quincy. A seemingly irrelevant similarity was all that was needed for residents of Quincy, Massachusetts, to feel a bond with the people of the homonymous town in Illinois.

Except that that seemingly irrelevant similarity was anything but irrelevant. It is a feature that is fundamental to human relationships and, as a consequence, human persuasion too. We like more and feel more connected to those with whom we share similarities. Yes, opposites sometimes attract. But birds of a feather flock together much, much more often. So central is this concept that, surprisingly, it is often true even if we hear that we share common features with people considered to be undesirable or even reprehensible.

After reading an account of Grigori Rasputin, the 'Mad Monk of Russia' and a man largely considered a scoundrel for using his religious position to exploit others, people were asked to rate how likeable this unsavoury character was. No surprise that most reported him to be distinctly unlikeable. But one group was much more favourable towards him. Why? They had been told by researchers at the beginning of the study that they happened to have the same birthday as Rasputin. In the context of shared similarities even the most evil of people seem a little less evil. Such is the power of similarity and the impact it has on our liking of others.

So what are the implications? Well, one thing we know from decades of research is that we are much more likely to say 'Yes' to those we like. And if the amount we like someone is strongly linked to how similar they are to us, then people are more likely to engage and be persuaded by us to the extent we demonstrate a commonality.

When psychologists sent surveys to a group of perfect strangers, some people also received a note from the sender, whose name was either similar or dissimilar to that of the recipient. For example, a person called Robert Greer might get the survey from someone named Bob Gregar, and a woman named Cynthia Johnston might get the survey from someone named Cindy Johanson. Others received a note from a sender with a non-similar sounding name. Those receiving the survey from someone with a similar-sounding name were nearly twice as likely to complete and return it compared to those who received a survey from a dissimilar name. None of the participants, when later asked, cited the similarity of the sender's name as the reason why they completed the form. It shows both the power and the subtlety of similar-sounding names as a cue that prompts people when deciding whom to like. And help.

But it's not only names that trigger similarities. Shared interests, similar values, common hobbies, comparable tastes: all these can be highlighted as potential similarities that, when genuine and authentic, increase the likelihood that two people will get along. This might arise at a job interview, on a dating website, or at an event. And with increased likeability comes increased connection and increased influence.

The lesson here is clear. The truly effective persuader makes time to seek out and bring to the surface genuine similarities that they share with others before they make their request. A couple of well-placed questions about an individual's background or interests or even a quick internet search to identify shared similarities between you and a new contact could see your persuasive skills take flight.

Do opposites attract? Of course they sometimes do. But the road to 'Yes' is often reached much more directly through similarities.

ON LIKING

The first step to getting someone to agree with you is, often, to make them like you. Increase this possibility by identifying your commonalities.

Do your preparation. Seek out similarities such as shared backgrounds, interests and experiences.

Be sure to highlight them before making your pitch or request.

13

COMPLIMENTING

It's not enough for someone to like you – find genuine ways to show that you like your listener, and make them feel seen

A friend once spent a significant part of a night out complaining to anyone who would listen about a work colleague who she clearly wasn't fond of. Words like obnoxious, stubborn and uncooperative featured prominently in her description. As the evening progressed and the red wine flowed, the language she used to describe her contempt for this abhorrent person became ever more colourful. And certainly shouldn't be repeated publicly. Any casual interjection from a member of the listening group that there must be *something* likeable about this colleague only served to trigger another tirade of hatred. The collective conclusion was that this guy wasn't getting on her Christmas-card list anytime soon.

You can probably identify. Although not inevitable, it is extremely likely that at some point during your life you will encounter someone who you don't click with but with whom it is necessary to interact. Whether it's a prying, overly fussy in-law or a difficult colleague, no matter how satisfying it might be to deride and disparage them to others a simple fact remains. Come tomorrow, you will still face the challenge of figuring out how to navigate your way through those unavoidable encounters. And in the case of our friend, with the unwelcome accompaniment of a blistering hangover!

So if you find yourself in such circumstances, what can be done?

The usual advice is to avoid or ignore such people. But this is often easier said than done, particularly if the person in question is a colleague who you work alongside or a customer who you need to keep on side. Fortunately, persuasion researchers have identified another potentially useful strategy. Granted, it is a strategy that is much trickier than just avoiding the person in question. It is also somewhat counterintuitive and even, perhaps, brave. Because it requires you to look for something likeable about the very individual you dislike. And then tell them.

One reason why this approach, while effective, can be tough to implement is because we typically find it much harder to offer compliments to people for whom we harbour negative feelings. It's usually easier to generate reasons that support our current points of view than find ones to oppose them. However, if you have reached a point where anything is worth a try, then there are two steps you need to undertake to employ this strategy effectively.

First, it is necessary to recognise that, despite what you may think or have been told about them, everyone (yes, even them!) has at least one redeeming quality or characteristic. As difficult as it might be to imagine, someone somewhere probably likes them, admires them and loves them. Second, having identified that redeeming quality or character-istic, you need to find a way of mentioning it. Here, it is important to note that what you're after doesn't necessarily have to be a likeable feature about the person themselves (which might be just as well in the case of some people). A compliment about their approach to work, a previous success they have had, or even something admirable that they do in their personal life can suffice. It can be surprising to find out how an individual who acts like an objectionable, narcissistic, loathsome oaf when they are in the office also happens to be a dedicated charity worker, a great cook or a devoted son in their spare time.

It would be foolish to claim that a strategy that advocates identifying something likeable about someone you dislike and then telling them will lead you onto the road of 'Best Friends Forever'. But it can certainly help to reduce tensions, which might lead you towards the road of persuasive success. Why? Because by looking for likeable features in others we might come to discover something important: that they are (at least in some contexts) actually likeable. And we know from chapter 12, 'Liking', that people are generally more inclined to say 'Yes' to people who they like. And we are also especially likely to say 'Yes' to the people who tell us that they like us.

One study found that people were more likely to respond favourably to a colleague's request if that colleague had complimented them immediately before making the request. This increase in help occurred regardless of how likeable the requester was. It was the requester demonstrating their ability to see good in another, through the delivery of a compliment, which increased their persuasive success.

This is not an isolated example. Numerous studies have consistently shown how effective it can be to tell others that you like them and to give genuine compliments. Waiters receive increased gratuities after complimenting diners on their selection from the menu. Hairstylists get bigger tips after telling clients how much they like their new hairdo. And this holds true even when people know that the flatterer has an ulterior motive.

Of course, we are certainly not advocating disingenuous sycophancy or servility. But when done authentically a 'charm and disarm' strategy can provide an additional upside. Focusing on an admirable feature in someone you find difficult might actually lead to you genuinely liking them a bit more. A central source of our feelings about others is inferred from our actions. By considering likeable features in another person, not only do we reframe them in a positive way, but the act of verbalising praise, even for a difficult person, can influence a positive change in the way we perceive them.

So rather than using charm as a universal but rather blunt instrument of persuasion, the advice here is different. Look for genuinely likeable features in someone and find a way to include them when conversing with that person. But readers of *The Little Book of Yes* probably already knew that. You are, after all, a most discerning, intelligent and attractive bunch of people.

ON COMPLIMENTING

Before asking someone for something, think of one good thing about them, and include a compliment in your conversation.

This doesn't always have to be in the moment. Cultivate a positive relationship and use compliments generally. This can make people feel positive towards you so that when the time comes to ask a favour, they may be more likely to say yes!

14

LABELLING

Names and labels matter to people: use them wisely

A long time ago (about thirty-five years ago, to be exact), in a galaxy far, far away, Luke Skywalker gained the ultimate form of compliance: he persuaded Darth Vader to turn against the evil emperor, and in the process saved his own life as well as restoring hope and peace to the galaxy. Skywalker was able to achieve this impressive outcome by the use of a simple, yet powerful strategy that has long been studied by persuasion scientists.

The strategy Skywalker used is known in psychology as the labelling technique. It involves assigning a trait, attitude, belief or other label to a person before making a request of that person that's consistent with that label. In *Return of the Jedi* Skywalker turns to Darth Vader and says, 'I know there's still good in you. There's good in you, I can sense it.' At first glance it seems unlikely that these simple words alone could have planted the seeds of change in Vader's mind, but psychological research is quite clear. Assigning people labels can have a powerful effect on their subsequent actions.

Take elections, for example. Few would argue that an important duty of citizens in any democracy is to exercise their right to vote. For centuries wars have been fought and millions have died in the pursuit of the right for every voice to be heard. Yet despite this, many millions still fail to vote on Election Day. To determine whether assigning a desirable label to people immediately after they confirmed that they intended to vote would have any effect on whether or not they actually *did* vote, researchers in the US conducted a rather interesting experiment. A large number of potential voters were interviewed and asked whether they planned to vote on Election Day in 2008 when Barack Obama and John McCain were running for president. Half of them were then told that, based on their responses, they could be characterised as 'above-average citizens who were indeed likely to vote'. The other half were informed that they were 'about average' when it came to their beliefs and behaviours.

The researchers then measured the turnout rates of each group and found that those who were labelled as 'good citizens' not only came to see themselves as 'good' citizens more than did those labelled 'average', they were also 15 per cent more likely to vote in the election that was held one week later.

It turns out that the labelling strategy isn't just effective in political domains or, in the case of Luke Skywalker, when deposing an evil emperor. There are many ways in which this technique can be used in your own persuasive pursuits. Imagine, for example, that you have someone at work who is falling behind, meaning that a project you are working on together is behind schedule. Imagine further that a couple of other colleagues have been less than helpful by assigning exactly the *wrong* kinds of labels to the worker who is struggling. 'She's always late delivering to deadlines' or 'He is so unreliable, you can never trust him to deliver when he says he will.' As a result, this team member's confidence in their ability to perform is dwindling fast.

A useful approach, assuming of course that you believe them to be capable of the task, is to remind them how hard-working and persevering they are. You could even point out examples of previous times when they have triumphed over similar challenges and successfully delivered. Once you have done this it is important that you then clearly assign a positive and helpful label to them that is consistent with your feedback. 'That's why I know we will be able to turn this round and deliver on time. I've always regarded you as a reliable and dependable person.'

Or perhaps you want to persuade one of your friends to join you on that backpacking trip or accompany you to a mud-soaked music festival weekend. If you do, then it may be a good idea to remind them, before making your risk-taking request, of what an adventurous and open-minded person they can be. Sometimes it isn't even necessary to label someone with a desirable trait. It can be enough to simply encourage them to 'self-label' by arranging for them to confirm that they do in fact possess such desirable traits. When researchers asked people 'do you consider yourself an adventurous person who likes to try new things?' before asking them to try a new soft drink, 76 per cent of people agreed to try it. This is impressive when you consider that without this self-labelling question only 33 per cent sampled the drink.

Other research has found that asking people 'do you consider yourself to be a helpful person?' before asking for their help on a task improved compliance from 29 per cent to 77 per cent. It seems that asking questions that direct people to purposefully probe their memories for times when they have behaved in a way that is consistent with the request you are about to make can sometimes be enough to motivate them. And it works when you are sculpting desirable behaviours in adults and children alike. For instance, our research has found that when teachers told children that they reminded them of other students who care about good handwriting, the kids spent more time practising their handwriting. And the practising continued even when the children thought that no one was around to watch.

Of course, there is always a 'Dark Side' to persuasion. One where the strategies outlined in this book might be used for evil rather than good. As tempting as this may be, we would only ever advocate their ethical use. So when it comes to labelling others, be sure to only assign the traits, attitudes, beliefs and actions that genuinely reflect your persuasion target's natural capabilities, experiences and personality. And that you want to encourage. But we are confident that you would never stoop so low or resort to such tricks in pursuit of evil ends.

After all, we sense much good in you.

ON LABELLING

Get into the habit of genuinely labelling people with the sort of traits that are consistent with the request you are about to make.

Be careful with negative labels, though. Don't be surprised if bemoaning your friend's tardiness makes her even later next time you go out together.

If possible, recall a time when you've been labelled positively by someone else (as hard-working, say) and remind yourself of its beneficial effects.

15

REASONING

Always give the reason behind your request

Convincing your children to do their homework instead of watching TV is no easy task. Neither is persuading a partner to do the washing up, requesting that your housemate takes their turn putting out the recycling, or pleading with a stranger to allow you to jump ahead in the security queue when you are about to miss a flight.

When facing such challenges you won't be surprised to learn that having a legitimate reason for why you are making your request is important. But you may be surprised to learn that there is something even more vital to your success. It is a single word that can dramatically increase the chances that people will say 'Yes' to you.

The word is *because*.

The persuasive power of *because* was first identified in a classic psychology study conducted in the 1970s by the wonderful Harvard psychologist Ellen Langer. Her research examined the circumstances under which people would be willing to allow a complete stranger to push in front of them in a queue.

Langer's chosen environment to conduct her research? A busy office, specifically, by the photocopy machine.

In her first experiment, Langer arranged for someone who was part of the study, and a complete stranger to those to whom they were speaking, to approach whoever was next in line to use the photo-copier and simply ask, 'Excuse me, I have five pages, may I use the Xerox machine?' When faced with this rather direct request, six out of ten people said yes. If this 60 per cent compliance rate surprises you, then recall that a key insight in chapter 9, 'Asking', is the fact that people are generally more likely to say yes to requests than we would ordinarily predict. This is something that Langer clearly recognised. She also recognised something else. When the stranger's request was followed with a reason – 'Excuse me, I have five pages, may I use the Xerox machine because I'm in a rush?' – compliance jumped to 94 per cent. So it would appear that one way to significantly increase the likelihood that people will say 'Yes' to you is to also state the reason why you are making your request.

But read on, *because* there's more. And it's something that's really fascinating.

In follow-on studies Langer didn't test merely the impact of accompanying a request with a reason. She also tested the specific reasons that were given, and found something quite bizarre. People were just as likely to say 'Yes' to strangers' requests even when the reason offered was completely meaningless!

Sometimes the stranger said: 'Excuse me, I have five pages. May I use the Xerox machine because I have to make copies?' Did people respond with, 'Duh! Of course you need to make copies. It's a photocopier!' Nope! Of those asked, 93 per cent simply said 'OK, go ahead' despite the fact that the reason given did not add any substantive, or even helpful, information.

It seems that, even though it is important that you *give* people a reason for making a request, it is even more important that you simply *have* a reason. And there is one word that is the single best one to use when it comes to signalling that you have a reason. That word is *because*.

The word *because* gets its persuasive power *because* we typically associate its use with good rationales that follow it.

- Please can I attend the supervisor training *because* it will put me in a better position to win a promotion?

- Please eat your fruit and vegetables *because* they are good for you.

  Advertisers in particular understand the persuasive power of the word *because*:

- *because* you're worth it (L'Oreal)

- *because* your best days start with breakfast (Kellogg).

Be aware, though, that the power of *because* does have limits. When Langer increased the size of the request to strangers from five copies to twenty, the willingness of people to say 'Yes' dropped dramatically. It seems that the word *because* alone is quite good for smaller requests but less so for larger ones. As requests get larger, so does the need to provide legitimate reasons that will validate the request. Or, maybe, an incentive?

In a much more recent set of studies, researchers looked at the influence of offering a financial incentive rather than a reason in order to persuade people to let them jump to the front of the queue. As you might expect, when people in queues were offered a cash payment to let a stranger jump in line, the more money that was offered, the more successful the queue-jumper was. But here was the surprise. Hardly anyone who agreed to let someone cut in line actually accepted the money. (Students were most likely to take the cash.)

It seems that the cash incentive directly represented the level of someone's need. The higher the incentive, the greater the need that was being communicated, and the more likely someone was to say 'Yes' without actually accepting the cash.

So it seems that what Langer discovered almost fifty years ago is as valid and important today as it has ever been. When persuading others to say 'Yes' to your requests, proposals and ideas, always be sure to accompany them with a strong rationale, even if you think the reasons are fairly clear.

The answer to convincing children to tidy their rooms, teens to do their homework, housemates to recycle, and partners to do the dishes is as simple as saying *because* and providing a reason.

ON REASONING

Before you ask someone for something, make sure that you are clear why you are asking for it. And then make sure that they know too.

To work out your reason, ask yourself: 'What benefit will be gained as a result of my request?'

Make sure that you use the word 'because' during your request, to flag up your reasoning.

16

COMMITTING

*To receive real commitment to your requests, emphasise
quantifiable, public goal-setting*

When Boris Johnson was Mayor of London he
famously remarked that 'it's easy to make a promise.
The hard work is keeping them.' Not the most reassuring statement to hear from a political perspective,
but from a persuasion perspective his words do convey
a somewhat harsh truth. All too often we find that the
haste to which people will commit to a task is rarely
matched by a swiftness in delivering it. When it comes
to repaying that favour, promising that report or putting
up those shelves there is often a gap (and sometimes a
gulf) between someone promising to do something and
them getting round to actually doing it.

There is a pretty simple reason why. Committing to
doing something and actually doing it are two entirely

different things. Consider the New Year, a time when many of us will make quite a few commitments. 'To be healthier' or 'Do more exercise' are two common goals that we set. Notice that they are not only common commitments, made by many others, but are also common commitments made to ourselves: it is remarkably easy to forget that last year's resolution was practically identical to this year's. It's easier still to forget its tragic fate.

If this sounds familiar, you are not alone. Some of the media have even given it a name. A few years ago, Steve Martin, one of the authors of this book, was interviewed by the BBC for a feature entitled 'Death of a Diet Day'. It followed a large-scale UK survey that found that by 1 February almost 80 per cent of people had abandoned the New Year's Resolution they had been so motivated by just a few weeks before. It turns out that habitual behaviour is difficult to change. This is true whether we are attempting to persuade ourselves or others. Fortunately, there is a large body of social psychological research that reveals that a series of small adjustments to the way commitments are both made and monitored can significantly increase the 'stickiness' of that desirable change.

The first concerns ownership. When persuading others, and ourselves for that matter, to live up to commitments, those that are made voluntarily are significantly more likely to stand the test of time. As the saying goes: 'Those who act against their will, are of the same opinion still.' Humans typically have a strong preference for consistency. We strive to live up to our beliefs, values and self-ascribed traits. Framing a commitment that you want someone to make as consistent with their beliefs, values and self-ascribed traits usually makes it easier for people to sign up willingly, rather than, as is often the case, feeling like they have been coerced.

Voluntary commitments are all well and good but long-lasting commitments are those that are typically made actively and publicly. Gaining active and public commitments from colleagues, friends and family members reduces the likelihood that they might back out in the future.

As an example, consider those appointment reminder cards that are commonly distributed by doctors, dentists and hairdressers. Who writes down the date and time of your next appointment – you, or the chatty receptionist? In a study we led, which was conducted in GP surgeries, we measured the impact of asking patients to write down the date and time of their next appointment themselves, rather than a receptionist doing so. The number of people who missed appointments was 18 per cent less in the group that wrote down their own appointment time compared with those whose card was completed by the receptionist.

It seems that people are more likely to *live up* to what they actively *write down*.

So writing down, and describing in detail, voluntary, public actions can make a difference when it comes to turning a 'commitment to do something' into 'actually doing something'. Asking members of your team to write down their goals can help strengthen their commitment to those goals. A gentle reminder to flatmates about what they have said in the past about the flat being clean and tidy might be a more effective route to a dust-free home than threats, coercion or an outward burst of frustration. And, in the same way that Brownies and Scouts groups make a pledge to all members and then receive a badge which serves as a public reminder of their commitment, posting your goals and commitments on Facebook in a way that gains the support of followers and friends could mean the difference between eating biscuits or broccoli on 2 February.

On the topic of setting goals, received wisdom is to set a single, specific-number goal in order to focus your effort, or the effort of others. Lose 1 kilogramme in weight a month. Save £50 a month towards next year's holiday. Read two books a month. Give me three ideas by the end of the day. At first glance, this makes intuitive sense. Single-number goals are clear and concrete. But there are other factors at play when pursuing a goal. Two important factors are *challenge* and *attainability*. People want to feel sufficiently challenged by a goal. That way they can feel a sense of accomplishment when they reach the target. But if a goal becomes unattainable it is more likely to dishearten than motivate. And therein lies the problem with single-number goals. They are either relatively attainable, relatively challenging or, more likely, a compromise in between. There is an alternative, though.

It is called a *high–low* goal and it can be great for making sure that any task that you ask others to commit to stands the best chance of being sustained.

When researchers in a weight-loss club assigned one group a single-number goal of 'lose 2 pounds a week' and another group a high–low range goal that averaged the same ('lose 1–3 pounds a week') something very interesting happened. About half of those assigned a single-number weight-loss goal stayed in the programme for ten weeks. But nearly 80 per cent of those assigned the high–low range stayed in the programme. Perhaps most interesting of all was the fact that the high–low range goal had very little impact on overall performance. In fact, although not hugely significant, the data pointed to a slight performance advantage for those given a high–low range goal. So be assured that assigning yourself (or others) a high–low range goal won't just result in you achieving the lower end of the range. If anything, because high–low goals are maintained for longer, your performance is likely to be improved because of the extra time you dedicated to that goal.

ON COMMITTING

Next time you want someone to commit to something, give them a specific goal.

Bring up your commitments, or those of others, in public: at the pub, tell friends that your other mate has promised to go on holiday with you that summer; talk about your commitment to run a marathon on Facebook; promise that your team will deliver a project in a work meeting.

When setting goals for yourself, have in mind a range of outcomes that you'd be happy with, rather than a single one – you'll find that you'll strive for the best!

17

IMPLEMENTING

To encourage others to honour their promises, ask them to create a concrete plan for where, when and how they will do it

Most people will recognise Leonardo da Vinci for his iconic portrait, the *Mona Lisa*. But something that is probably much less recognised about the Renaissance polymath was that he was also a chronic procrastinator. When you are a genius of Da Vinci's magnitude you probably have plenty of ideas to get excited about. As a consequence many of his projects went unfinished or were abandoned altogether because his interest and attention got diverted to other intriguing ideas. Reflecting in his journal, he pondered, 'Tell me if anything ever was done. Tell me if *anything* was done.' Fortunately for us, many things were done. Including the most recognised painting in the world. Even if it took him close to sixteen years to finish.

Da Vinci is certainly not alone when it comes to putting things off for another day. Many of us can recall a colleague or friend assuring us 'Of course I can do that for you, leave it with me,' only for them to fall short when it comes to delivering. It is a fact of modern-day life that it's generally easier to commit to helping out in the future than to actually helping out. It's not necessarily that people are flaky. It's just that, compared to today, it is easy to kid ourselves that we'll have more time in the future than turns out to be the case. Like Leonardo da Vinci, something else comes up. Previous commitments get pushed down a rapidly expanding to-do list and many of the 'I'll do it tomorrow' tasks end up overlooked or forgotten entirely.

As a result, intentions can end up as distant cousins to implementations.

Recall how commitments are often more likely to become a reality when made voluntarily and publicly. But certainly not always – especially when there is a delay between someone signalling an intention and the time when they come to actually carry it out. In order to be ultimately persuasive, something else is needed to ensure that people will recall their commitments and, rather than put them off, actually complete them.

One way to do this is to use implementation intention plans. They work by asking people to create a concrete plan for where, when and how they will go about honouring something they have committed to doing in the future. By way of an example, think about voting. Most people agree that it is an important duty for citizens in a democracy to play a part in the process of electing representatives. Despite this, come Election Day, other things can easily get in the way of making it to the voting station. (Or maybe at the end of a busy day apathy simply sets in and civic duty gets crowded out by a welcome, and deserved, glass of wine.) Regardless, the result is that elections are often decided on a turnout of less than 60 per cent. This is exactly what researchers found when they phoned voters asking them if they were planning to vote in an upcoming election. Many people said that they intended to vote, yet they failed to show. But there was one group of voters who, after being asked if they intended to vote, were much more likely to do so. Why? They were also asked the time of day when they would vote and how they would get to the polling station.

It appears that to increase the chance of the requests we make of others being acted on, we need to ask people to consider and visualise specific concrete steps rather than just think about a broad, general goal. Whether this means that your children's intention to complete their homework is more likely to be realised if you get them to create an implementation plan is uncertain. But it may be a less wearying approach than the usual carrot-and-stick method.

No conversation about implementation would be complete without a focus on another individual who we frequently find it hard to persuade. Ourselves.

Whatever goals we set ourselves, from exercising regularly to being more productive at work, from behaving in a more environmentally conscious way to reducing the time spent on social media, there is much to be said for the If…When…Then… Implementation Plan.

Here is how it works. You pick a cue or situation that occurs at a regular and predictable time or place, or during an event, and you link a desirable action to that cue. For example, imagine that you want to persuade yourself to eat a little more healthily but your work often requires you to entertain clients. An example of an If…When…Then… Implementation Plan might be: '*If* I am out for a meal and *when* the waiter asks if I would like dessert, *then* I will order mint tea.'

Someone wishing to engage in regular exercise

might create an If...When...Then... Implementation Plan such as: '*If* it is Monday, Wednesday or Friday, *when* I get home from work, *then* I will go for a run.' This is not simply wishful thinking. In one study, nine out of ten people who made an implementation intention plan like this were more likely to be exercising regularly in the long term. This compares to only three in ten who made a broad and much less concrete plan.

If...When...Then... Implementation Plans are effective because, after some conscious effort, they begin to become habit. Once the plan is formulated, and the specified cue or situation is encountered, an associated plan of action stands ready to be activated. And when enacted frequently enough, the behaviour becomes routine.

One can only speculate as to whether Leonardo da Vinci himself would have benefited by having a few implementation plans in place. '*When* I am getting distracted by other ideas, *then* I will return to finishing the portrait.' Maybe some of those incomplete projects might have been turned into a few more masterpieces?

ON IMPLEMENTING

Remember that when creating a goal it may not be enough to just write that goal down on a to-do list.

Once you have identified a goal, create an implementation plan with specific steps about when, where and how you will deliver it.

When persuading others, encourage them to do the same. If you manage a team or are responsible for managing a project have regular implementation plan reviews.

18

COMPARING

What you compare an idea or request to can be as important as the idea or request itself

Imagine that you are in a competitive situation. Maybe you and your team are pitching for that new account. Or perhaps you are down to the last three in a battle for a dream promotion. Does the order in which you appear in the process have any influence on your likely success? For example, would being first up to bat increase your chances of success? Or would the odds be stacked more in your favour if you went last?

Take job interviews, for example. Like most candidates, you have prepared well. Refreshed your CV. Rehearsed and polished answers to the questions you are likely to be asked. Gathered up evidence and examples of how your previous experience and accomplishments make you the best candidate for the job.

But here is something you might not have considered. The order in which you are interviewed can have a significant influence on whether you get the job.

A few years ago an academic colleague was invited to an interview at a top university. The interview board explained that they would be seeing a number of candidates over the course of the day. Because the interviews were taking place in another city he was offered a choice of interview times to make his travel arrangements easier. Would he like to arrive the night before and be the first candidate the next morning? Or would he prefer a later slot so that he could travel in and out in one day? He chose to go first, presumably thinking that doing so gave him the chance to make a strong and lasting impression that subsequent candidates would struggle to match. Unfortunately, his plan didn't work. He didn't get the job.

Maybe he had a bad day. Or perhaps there were more suitable candidates. Regardless, the experience persuaded him to dig a little deeper into the psychology of job interviews – and what he found was astonishing.

Reviewing a random selection of interviews conducted over a five-year period at a world-renowned university, he observed that the last candidate almost always got the job. Believing that this was probably just a quirk of the academic world he looked at research in other competitive situations and found similar patterns. Performers who appeared towards the end of the Eurovision Song Contest were given higher scores by judges and were more likely to win. The same holds true for *American Idol* and *The X Factor*. Could it be that in competitive performances where people are being assessed, like job interviews, sales pitches and talent contests, judges' memories of candidates early in the process simply fade? If that's the case, then situations where candidates are evaluated after each individual performance should eliminate the effect. But that is not what happens. It is something else that causes this. And, surprisingly, it has less to do with the candidate's performance and much more to do with the order in which they appear.

People rarely make decisions in a vacuum. Choices are inevitably influenced by the context in which they are made. These contexts might include things like potential alternatives, the physical environment, and what someone is thinking about in the moment before a decision is made. As an example, think about choosing a glass of wine in a restaurant. A £5.50 glass seems expensive if it appears halfway down a list that begins with a house wine priced £3.75. However, it will appear much more reasonably priced if a £9 glass of wine appears on the list first. Nothing changes about the wines, just the order in which they are presented.

Make no mistake, the order in which options are presented has a huge influence on how people make comparisons and on what they subsequently choose. Suddenly, job interviews can be seen in a different light.

If you are one of a number of candidates, don't make the mistake of thinking that by going first you are not being compared to anyone. You are. Except that it's probably someone who doesn't exist. We're talking here about the job spec – the sheet of paper listing all the attributes of the perfect candidate. Selection panels are often stingier when evaluating the initial candidates, because they know that giving high marks to an applicant early in the process won't leave them any flexibility to reward higher scores to a better performer later. So, all other things being equal, if you are in a competitive situation with three or more candidates performing for a single opportunity our advice is: go last.

There are other ways in which you can subtly change the order of how things are presented in order to boost your persuasiveness. 'Always have a comparison' is the mantra of the accomplished influencer. It's important to think about what your influence target will be comparing your request or proposal to when they make their decision. Any favourable comparison you can introduce into the mix can increase the chances of your success. It can even make you (and your friends) more productive. Researchers found that people who were assigned six tasks to complete were much more likely to finish them if they were first told that a group of similar people were given ten.

So whether it's introducing a comparison that will be favourable to your proposal or request, or using existing contexts to your advantage, it pays to consider what your audience will be comparing your proposal to in the moment they make their decision.

ON COMPARING

All other things being equal, in a competitive situation with three or more candidates, try to arrange to go last.

When preparing proposals or requests, always ensure that you think about a favourable comparison.

Think about what or who your listeners will be comparing you with – and make sure you give them a more favourable alternative.

19

FOLLOWING

People will follow others' lead – so make sure that you highlight those whom you've already persuaded

When was the last time you encountered a situation in which you had to make a decision but weren't really sure what the right decision was? It is a fact of modern-day life that we often have to make choices without knowing what the right choice is. Another fact of modern life is that when making such decisions we are very likely to follow what others like us have done.

Airports are a good example. If you have ever found yourself joining a queue without being entirely sure if you are in the right one, you are not alone. We've all heard stories about people who arrive at an unfamiliar place – like an airport – and spend ages waiting patiently in line, only to find out when they reach the front that they are in the wrong queue, and get directed to the right (invariably shorter and faster-moving) one.

Restaurants are another good example. Among an array of eating options, do you choose the bustling restaurant that's full of people or the quieter one? In such uncertain situations the popular choice often prevails. If you do pick the quieter one, there's a good chance that they'll seat you at the front to make the restaurant *appear* busier. Or maybe you booked your restaurant in advance. Did the fact that one establishment had more four and five-star reviews than the others influence your decision? Most likely it did. In situations where people are uncertain of the correct course of action or where risk is involved, following the behaviour of others is often a reliable means to an efficient and quick decision. Psychologists call this 'social proof' – in other words, we will often follow the actions of those around us.

The persuasive power of this herd-like behaviour is well documented. One classic study looked at the effect of social proof on an individual's conformity. A group of people were asked which of three lines was the longest: A, B or C. The correct answer was clearly C. Each member of the group (who were in fact part of the experiment) was asked, in turn, to declare their answers. Everyone said, incorrectly, that B was the longest. The real experiment was to see whether the person who was asked last and who wasn't in on the trick would say what they saw. Even though C was clearly the correct answer, most people gave the answer B, to conform to the majority.

So why do most of us, at some point, succumb to the pull of the crowd? One reason is that if many other people are already doing something then it is probably a sign that it is the right thing to do. If hundreds of people run out from a building shouting 'Fire' it's best to follow them. Similarly, if all our friends are talking about the latest movie, or are posting reviews about how much they love this book on social media, then it probably means that you'd like the movie or this book too. Following also helps us to fulfil two fundamental human needs – to connect with others and to gain their approval.

So when seeking to persuade others, the advice is to highlight the fact that many people are already doing what you would like *them* to do. At home, rather than trying to use logic to persuade your child to do something that they really don't want to do, such as eating their greens, instead point out how their friends are doing it. In the office, communicating how many people are already behind a new initiative can help the idea to catch on. And when trying to persuade your friends to choose a particular holiday resort, don't rely on your own powers of persuasion, but instead point to all the positive reviews that others who have already visited have posted.

It is important to remember that the most effective kind of social proof is that which comes from a source that most directly resembles those you are trying to persuade. To continue the holiday example, if the positive online reviews come from people who are dissimilar (in terms of age, gender or interests) to your group of friends then your persuasion attempt will be much less effective. However, if you select reviews posted by people exactly like your friends in terms of profile, age and interests then your attempt becomes much more compelling.

Recognise, too, that pointing out the entrenched nature of something that is undesirable can actually lead to more of the same. The spouse who is regularly told 'you always forget to put out the recycling' is unlikely to change anytime soon. Similarly, if everyone in the office says 'meetings never start on time around here' the chances that they suddenly will is diminished. So the lesson is to point out to people the action that you would like to see, and to emphasise how it is already practised by many people like them.

And be sure to watch out for how the behaviour of the majority can influence you and may even cause you to lose out on opportunities. Let's go back to the restaurant. Imagine that you have finished dinner with your group of friends and the dessert menu arrives. The conversation isn't showing any signs of dwindling so you decide to treat yourself to dessert but are torn between the lemon cheesecake and the crème brûlée. So you wait for someone else to order first and take a cue from them about what is a good choice. But the person who orders first passes on dessert, claiming that they are too full. Then a second person does too. Quickly, the rest of the table follows suit. Although there is nothing stopping you from ordering a dessert – in fact, you still want one – the norm set by the group would make you stand out. Reluctantly you refuse too.

While we are certainly not suggesting that it is always a case of monkey see, monkey do, it is worth remembering that the behaviour and decisions of those around us can have a powerfully persuasive pull on our own. Fine if that helps us to avoid danger, or choose the right holiday or movie. But, for some people at least, if it gets in the way of dessert then that might be a persuasive step too far!

ON FOLLOWING

Be sure to show how people in a similar situation to those you want to influence have acted.

People follow those most similar to themselves. So rather than using the testimonial you are most proud of, use the one that comes from someone most like your influence target.

Build 'follows' on your social networks by highlighting your increasing number of followers. If your followers have risen from two hundred to four hundred you could tweet about the fact that the number has doubled; on Instagram, offer an incentive for your followers to help you reach a certain number.

20

LOSING

*Because losses weigh more heavily than gains, highlight
to your listener what they stand to lose*

Imagine that on your way to the office one day you
find a £20 note on the pavement. How happy would
you be? Like most people, after sparing a brief thought
for another person's misfortune in having dropped the
cash, you'll probably be quite pleased with your good
luck.

By way of contrast, imagine that instead of finding a
very welcome twenty quid on the pavement you get to
work and discover that it was you that lost the money!
How would you be feeling now? Pretty unhappy, we
would bet. Certainly much more unhappy about losing
the money than you would be happy about finding the
same.

The fact that most people are much more unhappy
at the thought of losing than they are happy at the

thought of gaining raises an intriguing question. If you were fortunate enough to find twenty pounds one morning only to lose it later that day would you be worse off? Obviously you wouldn't be economically worse off. The gain and the loss cancel each other out. However, emotionally, the chances are that you would feel much worse off. And this is for a simple reason well known to psychologists. Losses loom much larger in our minds than do gains.

One well-known study provides a neat demonstration. Households were provided with one of a pair of reports outlining a series of simple actions they could take in order to reduce their energy bill. The reports differed in just one way: half the households were told how much money they would save if they carried out the recommended actions, the other half were told how much they would continue to lose if they didn't. This small change in messaging had an impressive and immediate effect. Twice as many households took action when told what they would lose rather than what they would gain. The implications for persuasion are clear. Honestly pointing out to people what they stand to lose by not following your advice or recommendation can be a very effective strategy when it comes to spurring people into action and getting them to say 'Yes'.

The fact that most people are typically 'loss averse' can be particularly challenging when trying to persuade them to switch allegiances or change current habits and behaviours where it's not just about monetary losses. Switching from a favourite brand, attempting to give up a habit like smoking, or trying to eat a healthier diet all incur a different type of cost, in terms of familiarity, comfort, or, in the case of smoking, a diminished relationship with your fellow smokers; it may even involve a loss of face. For some, these are costs that are simply not worth paying. If you find yourself facing such a challenge, or are helping someone else face theirs, what can be done?

A good starting point is to realise that because people's mental exchange rate between losses and gains is more two-for-one than one-for-one, any suggested changes are unlikely to be effective if they offer only modest upsides to the status quo. So it will be important to clearly communicate how the alternatives provide significantly more advantages, and then frame those advantages as ones that are currently being lost.

Another important point to remember when persuading others is the scarcity value of your advice or recommendation. Pointing out to your audience what is genuinely rare and unique about your offer can be quite compelling. So your colleagues at work might be persuaded to help you out on a project if they are told of its unique benefits – perhaps even more so if they also come to learn that the team might miss out on its Christmas bonus if they don't all pull together. Similarly, a friend might be more likely to join you for dinner if they are told that it's the only evening you're free for the rest of the month. Adding that they will also miss out on a juicy new piece of gossip you have to share should seal the deal.

ON LOSING

Think about the things someone you want to persuade will gain if they say 'Yes' to your request. Now state those as things they could lose if they don't carefully consider your offer.

Use competition to increase your persuasiveness. If people come to know that your availability or services are in demand by others then these things become more attractive.

Value your time so that others will too. Don't say 'I'm free all day, you choose a time.' Instead say: 'I can meet on Saturday, either at four or seven.'

21

ENDING

If you want to have impact, and for people to remember you, make sure that you end on a high

Have you noticed how pop stars and other performers typically play their most popular songs or perform their best-loved acts at the end of their concerts, rather than at the beginning or during the middle? There is a reason. They know that their fans will go home feeling much happier as a result. Don't get us wrong, first impressions matter. Of course they do. But what happens at the end of an experience is usually much more important and certainly much more memorable.

As an example, imagine that one day you are asked to take part in an experiment about pain. For the first part of the experiment you are asked to place your hand in an ice-cold bucket of water for sixty seconds. It is an uncomfortable experience but you manage to endure it. Now comes the second part of the experiment. You are asked to place your other hand in the ice-cold bucket of water, again for sixty seconds. However, after the one minute has elapsed you are asked to keep your hand in the bucket for a further thirty seconds during which time the temperature of the water is increased by one degree centigrade. You are then asked which of these two experiences you would like to repeat. Would you like to endure sixty seconds of pain? Or sixty seconds of pain together with thirty seconds of additional, although slightly less extreme, pain?

Would you be surprised to learn that most people choose the latter? They actually choose to experience more pain. This makes no sense at all until you begin to consider that there are quite large differences between our actual experiences and what we remember about them. When we reflect on our experiences we seldom recall their entirety and instead focus on specific moments. And, when it comes to remembering our experiences, one moment in particular matters a lot more than the others: the ending. The water experiment is a nice demonstration of how we can endure quite a lot of discomfort and still look back favourably on an experience providing that things ended well. What it also demonstrates is how we tend to pay less attention to how long an uncomfortable experience lasts and, on some occasions, disregard its duration entirely. That probably explains why people in the 'ice bucket' experiment were willing to endure an extra 50 per cent of discomfort. As they reflected on their experience they disregarded the amount of time they were in pain and instead remembered that the second experience ended better than the first.

Examples aren't just limited to pop stars and their songs, or psychologists with their buckets of cold water. You can find them everywhere. The presentation at work that was going so well until someone split a jug of water on the laptop. An otherwise wonderful date that was marred because the waiter was rude at the end of the evening. A relaxing weekend away with a loved one spoiled by a delayed return journey or cancelled flight. Notice that these unfortunate endings do nothing to impact on the experience itself. Until the waiter was rude or the airline cancelled the flight, you were having a perfectly wonderful time. What is impacted is your memory of those experiences. With that in mind, making subtle changes to the way experiences end is important when it comes to engaging others.

If you want to have fabulous memories of your next vacation, rather than spreading your budget thinly by booking lots of small excursions and day trips, you'll be much better off spending a bigger chunk of your budget on one or two amazing experiences that you should schedule towards the end of your holiday. And if you are going to treat yourself by upgrading to a nicer seat, remember that you'll probably have much happier memories if you travel *back* in style instead of upgrading on the flight out.

The same is true when it comes to the conversations and interactions you have with others. How they end can have a significant influence on how happy others feel about us. So if you need to have a difficult conversation with a friend or family member, have the tough chat early and then arrange for something more pleasant to be talked about or an activity that can be shared and enjoyed together at the end.

As your favourite aunt would advise, never go to bed on an argument.

ON ENDING

Try to save the best news until last. It will have a much bigger impact on people.

When presenting, ask yourself 'what do I want people to remember most?' and offer that at the end.

Make a point of reminding yourself and your team members of the good times. It is easy to forget great times that have been shared – especially if some of them didn't end so well.

THE SCIENCE OF
PERSUASION

As a team of persuasion scientists it is important to us that we only present ideas, offer insights and make recommendations that have been informed by scientific evidence. No guesses, hunches or intuitions. Only ideas and principles that have been proven to increase the chances of someone's persuasive success.

The Little Book of Yes refers to a number of such studies. Some were conducted by one or more of us, while many more were conducted by other social and behavioural scientists. It is standard practice to cite all the references in full-size books. As *The Little Book of Yes* has purposefully been designed to be, well, little, instead of including multiple extra pages of scientific references we have made them available online. Readers interested in a more detailed understanding of the studies we cite should visit www.littlebookofyes.com where they will find a full list of references along with links to the original scientific papers.

ADDITIONAL READING AND RESOURCES

Readers interested in learning more about influence and persuasion might like to explore this short list of recommended books – they are all excellent points of entry to the wider world of persuasion, and also offer useful insights into how to influence and persuade others (and yourself, too). (And yes, some of them are written by us.)

Dan Ariely, *Predictably Irrational* (Harper Collins, 2009)

Dale Carnegie, *How to Win Friends and Influence People* (Vermilion, 2006)

Robert B. Cialdini, *Influence: Science and Practice, Fifth Edition* (Pearson, 2008)

Robert B. Cialdini, *Pre-Suasion: A Revolutionary Way to Influence and Persuade* (Random House Business, 2017)

Adam Galinsky and Maurice Schweitzer, *Friend or Foe* (Random House Business, 2016)

Noah Goldstein, Steve Martin and Robert Cialdini, *Yes! 60 Secrets from the Science of Persuasion* (Profile Books, 2017)

Chip Heath and Dan Heath, *Made to Stick* (Arrow Books, 2008)

In addition, readers of *The Little Book of Yes* might like to view our popular ten-minute YouTube video which explains the key principles of influence and persuasion. Simply search #scienceofpersuasion

You may also like to visit our website: www.influenceatwork.co.uk